MODERN SHOESTRING

MODERN SHOESTRING

CONTEMPORARY ARCHITECTURE ON A BUDGET

Susanna Sirefman

The Monacelli Press

To the most amazing people I know—Sarah, Penelope, and
as always, Zander

Thank you to all the architects and designers whose work is
included in this book for their time and materials. Thank you
to the many photographers who have allowed us to publish their
spectacular images. An enormous thank you to all the forward-
looking clients of the projects featured here: without pragmatic
dreamers these wonderful homes would never have been built.

I am grateful to Andrea Monfried for inviting me to write
again for The Monacelli Press and for sharing my enthusiasm for
this book's important topic. I also wish to thank Stacee Lawrence
for her graceful editing and mutual understanding of my vision
for this book, and Elizabeth White for her careful and expert eye,
and mgmt. for their elegant design.

And a special thanks to my daughter Sarah, whose first-grade
editing checklist came in handy while writing this book and who,
along with her sister and their dad, make everything in life
so very special.

First published in the United States of America in 2008 by
The Monacelli Press, Inc.
611 Broadway, New York, New York 10012

Copyright © 2008 by The Monacelli Press, Inc.
Text © 2008 by Susanna Sirefman

Library of Congress Cataloging-in-Publication Data
Sirefman, Susanna.
Modern shoestring : contemporary architecture on a budget / by Susanna Sirefman.
p. cm.
ISBN 978-1-58093-202-8 (hardcover)
1. Architecture, Domestic—United States—21st century.
2. Dwellings—Design and construction—Cost effectiveness. I. Title.
NA7208.2.S57 2008
728'.370973–dc22
2007044732

Printed in Italy

Design by mgmt. design

CONTENTS

THE NEW LUXURY: BESPOKE BARGAINS

The intimate scale and specific program of domestic architecture has historically provided a rich testing ground for architectural innovation, resulting in many very beautiful, very modern homes. Yet there is a common misconception that the commission and construction of a contemporary house will cost the owner a fortune. This is not true. A sexy, custom-designed house need not break the bank, as the eighteen projects showcased here demonstrate. In fact, tight budgets often serve as a catalyst for exploring nontraditional materials and innovative construction techniques.

This volume offers a savory sampling of the possibilities for budget-minded construction. The dwellings featured, freestanding single-family homes completed between 2002 and 2007, were chosen for their moderate prices and their fine, holistic design. Functionalism and a modern aesthetic were of particular importance. Several variables affecting the construction costs that are nearly impossible to tabulate have been omitted: the cost of inflation over time, regional differences in the prices of materials, architects' fees, and the purchase price of land. Turnkey prefabricated houses were not included, due to the fact that mass-produced prefab can never truly engage the idiosyncrasies of a specific site.

This book is organized around the construction cost of each house, opening with the least expensive, in Lubbock, Texas, at an incredible $51 per square foot, and ending with a remarkably cost-effective residence in Echo Park Hills, California, built for $220 per square foot. It is no surprise that projects in Florida and California, with their extensive geotechnical code requirements, and New York, one of the country's most expensive places to build, fall at the higher end of this range. Nevertheless, these figures are remarkable in light of an informal survey revealing that the construction cost per square foot of a typical high-end, architect-designed house almost anywhere in the United States usually starts at $400 per square foot and, depending on client requests and materials, may reach as much as $2,000 per square foot.

Considered collectively, the homes here represent a new trend in forward-looking, inventive architecture and a new definition of luxury: the comfort and specificity of custom design without the high price tag. All houses were tailor-made by either licensed architects or designer-led architect teams. The site context, layout, materials, construction process, and detailing were planned to meet the specific needs, desires, and budgets of specific people, not speculative inhabitants, and beautifully reflect the distinctive individuality of each owner. Working with an architect or designer can be a magical experience, and there is no reason that those with limited funds should not be privy to that process or product—a bespoke home.

TOPICAL MODERNISM

The houses here can all be labeled topical modernist houses in that they are conceived and composed with a sense of linear rigor, clean—but not spartan—streamlined spaces, pragmatic flow, precise detailing, and an established relationship between inside and outside. They succeed where other designs have failed because they are both elegant and comfortable. None of these houses proposes to be a universal solution. Each architect allows client needs and the unique dialogue between building and site to inform the architectural language of the design, establishing a clear relationship to location, culture, and inhabitants.

The idea of the inexpensively built house has been met with some skepticism in the history of American modernist architecture. Although modernist domestic architecture in America took root in the early 1920s in California, as a movement it was not officially "introduced" until the 1932 exhibition titled *Modern Architecture—International Exhibition* at the Museum of Modern Art in New York, which was curated by Henry-Russell Hitchcock and Philip Johnson. Americans were ready to celebrate new possibilities for glass, steel, and concrete, but the movement's tenets relating to social responsibility, heavily emphasized by its European practitioners, were never fully embraced here except as they pertained to mass-produced housing.

A number of prominent architects including Irving Gill, William W. Wurster, Rudolf Schindler, and Richard Neutra designed spectacular, expensive houses following the formal rules of modernism. Many modernists, however, were not interested in creating one-off, custom-designed houses. Prototypes for mass production were often developed both here and abroad. In fact, many of the greatest European modernists, including Walter Gropius and Le Corbusier, designed steel "worker" homes capable of being reproduced in vast numbers. In the 1930s Frank Lloyd Wright designed roughly fifty similar, small, L-shaped houses intended for middle-income families, known as the Usonian houses, which partly inspired the explosion of pragmatic, long, low, inexpensive suburban ranch houses in the 1950s. Wright's student Robert Anshen of Anshen & Allen, along with A. Quincy Jones, also designed prototypes in 1949 for Joseph Eichler's famous developments of affordable modernist homes in California.

Many aspects of contemporary American culture are perceived as falling into two polarized camps: intellectual, hoity-toity pursuits or plebeian activities. Classical music is pitted against pop music, serious literature against beach reading, the allegedly highbrow *New York Times* against the layman's *Post*. It is a peculiar phenomenon that, comfortable in one sphere, we do not often seek out the value in the other. This prejudice has permeated our design culture for years. Products ranging from home furnishings to clothing are often either expensive and well-designed or cheap and unattractive. Recently, the design world has tried to bridge this gap by embracing a third genre: highly conceptual and inexpensive mass-produced products. But the underlying plutocratic message is still that the masses can have a well-designed object only if they all have the same well-designed object. Just think Alessi versus Target, Carolina Herrera versus H&M.

It is an astounding fact that, despite the initial popularity of modernist developments around the country, there remains very little interest in constructing houses of a topical modernist bent on a large scale. Today pseudo-Palladian and bloated Spanish Colonial McMansions reign. All the more reason why many architects and designers are interested in working on custom modernist houses that are affordable and will be appreciated and valued for their uniqueness.

MORE IS MORE MODERNISM

The eighteen projects here do not save money by using less space or material. Instead, they squeeze as much usable living space out of a budget as possible. Featured projects run from a modest 1,200 square feet to a massive 5,000 square feet. The average is 2,283 square feet, a wee bit larger, in fact, than the Census Bureau's current national average of 2,248 square feet for newly completed single-family homes. According to the National Association of Home Builders, the average square footage of a new single-family home in 2004 was 2,349 square feet. By 2006, the American Institute of Building Design, a national organization that promotes the use of qualified specialists in residential design, reported that this average had reached 3,420 square feet. Considering that the 1950 average was 983 square feet, the growing trend for ever more space is clear.

Many of the projects derive their spaciousness from strategic front-end planning and a focus on thoughtful and adventurous building techniques. Christoff:Finio Architects saved on construction costs and gained extra living space by hanging the floors of a new townhouse in Brooklyn from the existing walls of the buildings on either side rather than erecting new freestanding walls. This solution, simple in hindsight, was actually a highly creative and unusual approach that allowed the budget to accommodate a total of 4,200 square feet. Perhaps the most dramatic examples are those of Bates Masi Architects and Single Speed Design. Paul Masi composed the Upcher House in East Hampton around a commercial shelving system of adjustable steel columns, brackets, and arms that are more stable than traditional timber-frame systems and support the owner's extensive, weighty book collection. The entire structural system cost merely $7,000. This solution opened up the floor plan and allowed the modest budget to accommodate two stories. Single Speed Design constructed the Big Dig House, a pioneering architectural experiment, with recycled parts taken from the temporary infrastructure required to build Boston's Central Artery/Tunnel Project. Reclaimed materials were used primarily as found, not only saving money so that the owners could afford the final 3,800-square-foot house, but—equally as important—saving 600,000 pounds of steel and concrete from becoming landfill.

Modernists also focus on a clear pattern of circulation, allowing for every possible corner to be functional by eliminating dead ends and decorative niches. In the 18th Street House and F10 House, stairs are cleverly stacked to one side, creating a remarkably efficient layout and maximizing usable floor area in the narrow spaces. Fluidity of the domestic program is another important element. Greg Chasen's 1,700-square-foot Duane Street Residence in Los Angeles reallocates space initially allotted for an indoor garage to a spacious home office, and leaves the car outdoors. Similarly, Urs Peter Flueckiger converted the intended garage on his house to an art studio for his wife, and architect Byron Mouton, who led the design effort for Prototype-01, created a house that can be converted into a duplex to accommodate a multigenerational family, two families, or additional live/work space. Our resourceful heritage has made us a pragmatic country. Homebuilders will frequently construct a home without a professional designer or licensed architect leading the project. But it is often false economy to design a home, however small or simple it may seem, without careful consideration and a design professional. Although each of the featured projects is thoroughly contemporary, their high architectural standards are notable, fresh interpretations of the clean, precise, and rational tenets of modernism.

DREAM CLIENTS

Historically, the production of original houses has required an enlightened patron interested in architectural experimentation. There are many well-known examples, such as the Robie House in Chicago, designed by a young Frank Lloyd Wright in 1908. The home was commissioned by a wealthy 27-year-old entrepreneur who gave Wright complete freedom to test new materials and forms. In 1928, the modernist giant Mies van der Rohe was also given a wonderful opportunity to explore progressive ideas with the commission for a private residence from Fritz and Greta Tugendhat in the Czech Republic. Today, fantastic contemporary residences in this same tradition continue to be built around the globe, most commonly commissioned by wealthy, adventurous clients. The projects featured here differ only in their process—

and perhaps finishes—from these high-end showpieces. Their patrons all share a liberal vision, an understanding of the value of the design process, and a passion for making quality homes that are comfortable and functional for real families.

Unlike their wealthier counterparts, the owners of these custom homes often had to contribute to the process physically to bring projects to completion on budget. Many different cost-cutting techniques were employed, sweat equity being the most common. The owners of Cavehill Residence, for example, cut their budget in half by doing almost all the demolition and building themselves, a brave move considering that they had no prior experience. The trade-off was that the project took twice as long as if the couple had hired a contractor, but their enthusiasm and energy enabled them to own a home that they could not have afforded otherwise.

In addition to taking advantage of architects' suggestions for installing ready-made, low-cost materials in creative ways, shopping personally for discarded custom orders or watching for bargains at auction houses also cut costs for many of these homeowners. Commercial windows, industrial hardware, and galvanized or corrugated metal are some of the most popular money-saving inclusions. Christoff:Finio Architects found that installing aluminum-magnesium commercial railings as banisters and using institutional baseboard heaters was cheap and also fit their Brooklyn townhouse's loftlike industrial style. In the Newfield House, Central Office of Architecture chose a strong, stainproof, black epoxy-resin frequently used in medical laboratories for the long countertops throughout the house.

Conversely, at William Massie's Milan House in upstate New York, the owner decided to make other sacrifices in order to incorporate custom structural components. The architect designed exterior and interior surfaces—wood, metal, and acrylic—with an unusual computer-driven fabrication technique that essentially formed them into oversized jigsaw puzzle pieces

at a state-of-the-art laser-cutting workshop in Detroit. These materials were designed expressly for the building's craggy forest perch and the intimate, classically hip ambience the owner desired. In all of these instances, the role played by the open-minded, involved clients in each project's success cannot be overstated.

THE PLEASURE OF THE PERFECT FIT

The construction of a home is an enormous financial investment, and through sheer will, originality, and an understanding of the importance of design, these homeowners garnered huge savings and acquired singular, individualized homes. There is no single, easy answer to great domestic design on a budget, but a plethora of avenues that can lead to achieving a unique, modern house for a relative bargain. With a little imagination, it is amazing what can be accomplished. As with anything in life, be it clothing, a partner, or a home, there is nothing more pleasing than a perfect fit.

HOUSE ON TWENTY-FIRST STREET
LUBBOCK, TEXAS
URS PETER FLUECKIGER
$51.00 PER SQUARE FOOT
2004

An unusual blend of discipline and whimsy defines this 2,750-square-foot house. Urs Peter Flueckiger, a professor of architecture at Texas Tech University, designed numerous iterations of this remarkably low-budget house for his own young family. "The process was miserable, but the final result is evidence that good ideas can make a big difference," he says. Flueckiger originally envisioned a two-story house with multiple skylights. Financial constraints led him instead to a one-story building clad in industrial-sized sheets of corrugated metal. The resulting shedlike structure is elegant in its simplicity and capacious enough to meet the needs of all family members. The cost of building the house was half that of an average home in the area.

Lubbock is known for its extremely flat topography, a natural attribute that was central to cost savings for the house since little site preparation was required. A dilapidated structure on the 50-by-150-foot lot was razed, but its electric, phone, and cable lines were kept. The traditional frame is constructed of 2-by-6-foot timbers set on a concrete slab. The corrugated-steel siding, painted cherry red by the owners, cost $2.50 per square foot; the steel used for the roof was only $1.50 per square foot. Six sets of sliding glass doors and the clerestory windows—a substitute for the skylights Flueckiger originally intended—lend a cushy, sophisticated feel to the structure and allow for natural ventilation. Materials were purchased in standard manufacturers' proportions, to take advantage of correspondingly low pricing. A pergola shades the sides of the house and the walkway along the lawn; its beams are steel and the canopy is bamboo purchased in rolls of 6 by 16 feet for $24 each at Home Depot. It was installed in one day.

The house's layout follows a traditional southwestern courtyard formation—every room opens onto a central outdoor space. Three bedrooms, two bathrooms, and a 40-foot-long room containing kitchen, dining, and living room spaces form the main body of the house. Two 440-square-foot studios—one for Flueckiger and one for his wife, a painter and art professor—flank this central living area. To minimize costs on interior details, the concrete floor is unadorned, and wire racks and metal footlockers are used in place of built-in closets. Flueckiger also designed and manufactured much of the Baltic-birch-plywood shelving and furniture. He fitted the kitchen with maple cabinetry, also of his own construction, which was less dear than having prefabricated cabinets installed.

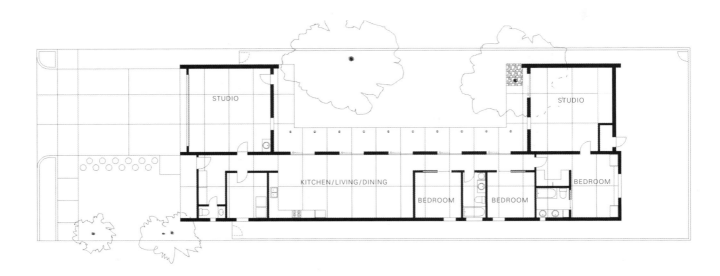

Bold color throughout lends a fresh, modern feel to this pragmatic project. Interior walls are enlivened by a vivid apple-green paint that complements the bright red exterior, and the cyanotype-blue interior doors are decorated with soft silhouettes of local mulberry leaves, softening the rigorous rectilinear lines of the house. Little of this playfulness is evident from the discreet street facade, however. The striated concrete-block front entrance is decidedly low-profile, helping the structure blend well with other eclectic homes in the neighborhood. The architect worked throughout to infuse the project with the clean, minimalist aesthetics of a personal hero, the artist Donald Judd, who also happens to have designed a house in Lubbock.

KEEL CABIN
WHITEFACE RESERVOIR, MINNESOTA
SALMELA ARCHITECT
$60.00 PER SQUARE FOOT
2006

Architects are frequently asked to design a house around a client's specific collection—usually paintings, photographs, books, glassware, or pottery. In this rather unorthodox case, Karl and Mary Keel requested that architect David Salmela design their house around a large assortment of bargain-basement windows. Over 40 overstock and slightly imperfect custom windows, skylights, and exterior doors purchased at a series of auctions were presented for inclusion, neatly cataloged in a spreadsheet documenting the shape and measurements of each. Salmela describes this as "an exciting design challenge. We managed to use up all the windows, including those that were odd little quarter circles and polygons." A few additional windows were purchased to maximize views of both the lake and woods, resulting in a building that has festive, eclectic fenestration.

The 1,650-square-foot cabin sits on a very private, insulated site on the Whiteface Reservoir. The property, a long-term lease from the Minnesota Power Company, was also secured at auction. The house itself is composed of two separate rectangular volumes, a two-story main dwelling and a one-story apartment for guests. These are connected by a large porch that is covered with a sloped, polycarbonate roof. Says Salmela: "We raised the house on concrete piers for minimum impact on the existing pine trees. It is a simple solution that is better for the earth." Elevating the building between 3 and 7 feet off the ground had an unexpected fringe benefit—eliminating the need for porch screens. Mosquitoes mainly hover near the ground.

The Keels and Salmela found creative ways to keep down costs on other construction and finish materials. They imported birch flooring from Russia through a discount Web site and salvaged slate blackboards discarded by the University of Minnesota for clever reinvention as kitchen and bathroom countertops.

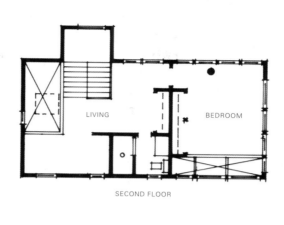

SECOND FLOOR

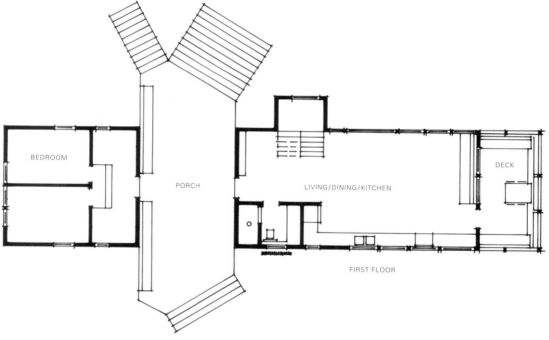

BEDROOM

PORCH

LIVING/DINING/KITCHEN

DECK

FIRST FLOOR

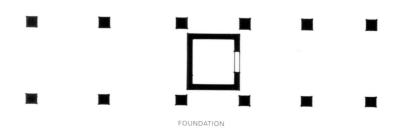

FOUNDATION

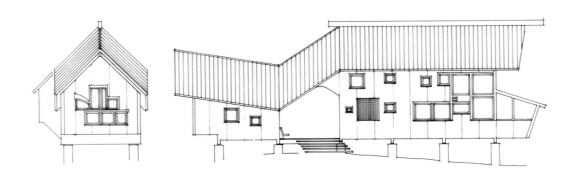

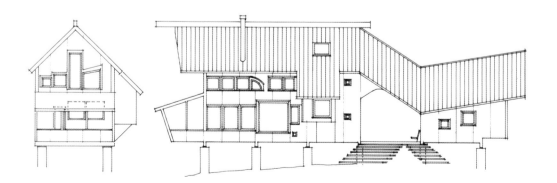

PROTOTYPE-01
NEW ORLEANS, LOUISIANA
TULANE DEPARTMENT OF ARCHITECTURE/URBANBUILD
$80.00 PER SQUARE FOOT
2006

After Hurricane Katrina, Reed Kroloff, then dean of the Tulane School of Architecture, founded the URBANbuild studio to aid in the reconstruction of New Orleans. He saw an opportunity to give students practical experience designing and constructing homes while simultaneously meeting an urgent local need for affordable housing. Kroloff describes the forward-looking program as "providing strong urban design strategies and apolitical master planning with no presumptions about the correctness of historical elements." Students and faculty—in partnership with Neighborhood Housing Services of New Orleans, UJAMAA, NeighborWorks America, MIT, BNIM Architects, and the Riggio family—concentrate on rehabilitating the neighborhoods most devastated by the storm in a manner that both respects and extends the city's legacy. This house, located in the Upper Treme in the Sixth Ward, was the first of the studio's four prototypes to be built.

Prototype-01 features a clean, modern exterior but also maintains demonstrable ties to the local vernacular. The house is conventionally framed using stick frame building methods, both to accommodate the students' experience with construction and to celebrate the area's traditional building techniques.

Newly enacted flood zoning requiring new buildings to be elevated posed a design challenge, since the team intended for the structure to fit seamlessly into the neighborhood. Clever manipulation of the section enabled the floor to be raised between 3 and 5 feet—exceeding the zoning requirements and matching the height to other houses in the vicinity. Materials such as galvanized roofing, concrete block, and sustainable cementitious board make the house both affordable and environmentally responsible. Free labor, provided by the students who erected the house as part of their course work, cut the project budget in half.

The house totals 1,370 square feet, with a floor plan for three bedrooms and two bathrooms, although it can be converted into a duplex to accommodate a multigenerational family, two families, or live/work space. The porch, an important regional element, mediates the elevation and provides a public face for the house. This funky reinvention of a typical New Orleans portico offers an inviting and playful space. Large double doors adjacent to the modest main entrance sport a checkerboard pattern of glazing in alternating panes of transparent and translucent glass. When open, they also allow passage directly into the dining area via a

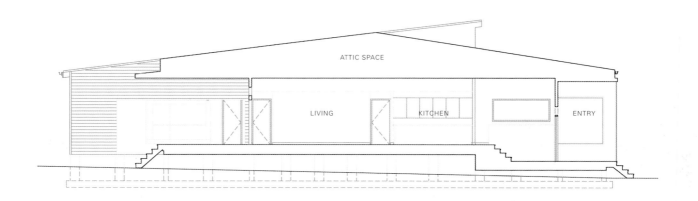

ATTIC SPACE

LIVING   KITCHEN   ENTRY

BEDROOM

BEDROOM   BATHROOM   CLOSET   BEDROOM

DINING   PORCH

LIVING   KITCHEN

long, treated pine step that doubles as a bench. Kroloff notes, "Houses here are tall and skinny with porches both at front and back. We wanted to study and learn from that rather than merely reproduce period homes. This house offers an affordable alternative for house design in the warm, moist climate of the Gulf South." In many ways, Prototype-01 is a truly modern home that has succeeded in improving on history.

NOLA MODERN
NEW ORLEANS, LOUISIANA
NODESIGN
$115.00 PER SQUARE FOOT
2007

The architects Gabriel Smith and Nicholas Marshall, founding principals of the firm nodesign, are so close they bought adjoining properties on which to build their respective family homes. The duo spent considerable time discussing and sketching elaborate shapes for their houses, all of which proved too expensive for them to build. While having coffee one day, Smith was struck by the humble, economical form of the sugar cube. Further research substantiated his hunch that it would indeed be a very efficient, very straightforward form for a domestic building. Because of the structure's small footprint and the minimal ratio of exterior skin to interior volume, it would also be considerably cheaper to construct than the complex forms he and Marshall had been exploring.

The architects placed two 32-by-32-by-32-foot cubes on the double lot as though it were one site, taking advantage of the shared yard, providing access to good views, and creating some privacy for each 2,000-square-foot home. One structure sits close to the street, while its neighbor has been pushed back 20 feet. This checkerboard arrangement means that one yard is shaded in the morning and the other in the afternoon, making the outdoor space more functional for both families. Similarly,

the yin and yang placement of the outdoor decks—in the rear of one house and in the front of the other—allows both families to enjoy more comfortable outdoor time than either would alone. Although the houses are nearly mirror images of each other, their fenestration differs due to the immense care taken in plotting the orientation of windows relative to the sun. The architects made models to study the effect its daily path would have on each room. Consequently, numerous windows were placed on the east side of each building, and walls that face west were left almost completely solid. No overhangs were required to shelter the houses from the brutal southern sun, which is unusual for New Orleans. This daylighting study helped to cut down on both construction and lighting costs. The architects and their families were obliged to move in before their electricity was hooked up, due to overwhelming service demands following Hurricane Katrina, and affirm that the houses successfully exploit the potential and drama of natural light. "It is like being in a ship, watching the sun move around. There is a lot of pink light that penetrates deeply into the floor plan," says Smith.

Nodesign followed a number of other economical procedures when planning and constructing these homes, including

fabricating almost all the cabinetry in their own workshop and, as a design/build project, erecting the two homes at the same time. While the buildings appear as solid steel cubes, the siding is Galvalume industrial metal attached to conventional framing. This material is 20 percent less expensive than steel stud framing and achieves an ultramodern, sophisticated, gleaming profile. Yet it was the geometry of the houses—simple, pure cubes—that turned out to be the biggest and stylistically smartest money-saving maneuver.

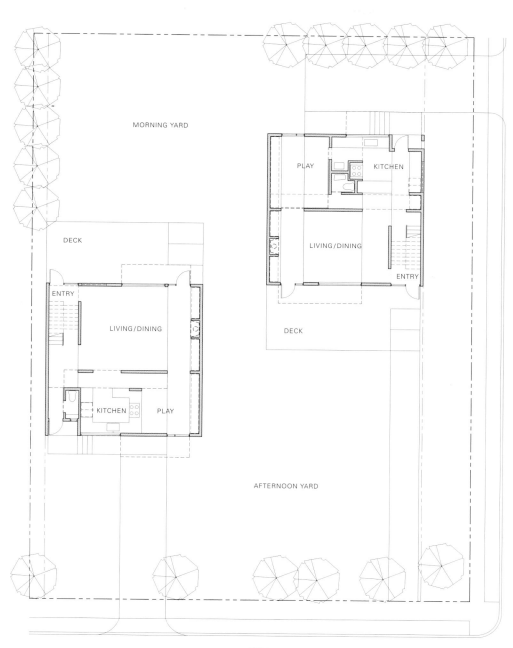

MORNING YARD

PLAY   KITCHEN

DECK   LIVING/DINING

ENTRY   ENTRY

LIVING/DINING   DECK

KITCHEN   PLAY

AFTERNOON YARD

SITE PLAN

CAVEHILL RESIDENCE
SEATTLE, WASHINGTON
EGGLESTON FARKAS ARCHITECTS
$120.00 PER SQUARE FOOT
2006

It took an enormous collaborative effort to construct this two-story, 1,700-square-foot house in Seattle's Queen Anne Hill neighborhood. The clients are friends of the architect, the contractor, and their spouses, and they all built this simple, boxy, modern house together. The owners, Michael and Eileen Thompson, recently relocated from their native Belfast, Ireland. By doing most of the demolition and construction themselves, they cut their construction budget in half; on the other hand, the intense do-it-yourself process took eighteen months—twice the time it would have taken a contractor to complete a job of this scope.

John Eggleston and his wife, an artist, taught the Thompsons basic carpentry, welding, and painting. In a rather unusual arrangement, the contractor would demonstrate a construction procedure and then assign tasks to the Thompsons, who performed the actual manual labor. They were responsible for site excavation, trenching, earthwork, demolition, mixing and pouring mortar, and installing modular siding, wood flooring, ceiling panels, and tiling. They used these freshly developed abilities to inform design decisions, determine material choices, and make selections for finish details. Skilled jobs such as structural framing, plumbing, final electrical connections, and installation of the hydronic heating system were left to the contractor.

In order to take advantage of grandfathered zoning rights, Eggleston Farkas decided to keep fragments of the existing foundation and some first-floor framing, which allowed the new street facade to come closer to the property line than current laws permit.

A new foundation was poured underneath the old, and the original hollow concrete block was further reinforced by infill. Code required a second-story setback, resulting in an outdoor sundeck with spectacular views of the Olympic Mountains and Puget Sound. Public spaces are found on the second floor in an open, loftlike arrangement. This fluid space encompasses the living, dining, and kitchen areas, and is sheltered under a butterfly roof that maximizes the fabulous panoramic view. The private quarters—bedroom, office, and bathroom—are on the ground level in a typical contemporary "upside-down" allocation of spaces.

Almost all the finish materials were purchased at a huge discount during visits to Home Depot or Boeing Surplus at odd

hours of the night. The most spectacular find was cream bathroom tile, a rejected special order that was marked down significantly. Salvaged, reinvented items also fill the house. The contractor provided a flat wooden door that went unused at a different job site; the Thompsons trimmed it with steel and transformed it into a dining table for an astounding $5. An old steel I-beam languishing in the Egglestons' backyard was cleverly repurposed as a kitchen backsplash.

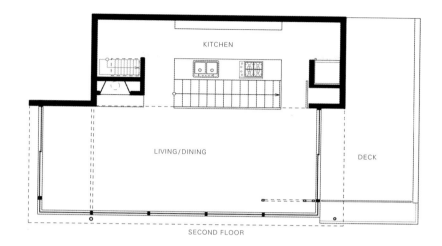

KITCHEN

LIVING/DINING

DECK

SECOND FLOOR

CLOSET/
DRESSING

ENTRY GALLERY

ENTRY PORCH

MASTER BEDROOM

OFFICE/GUEST

FIRST FLOOR

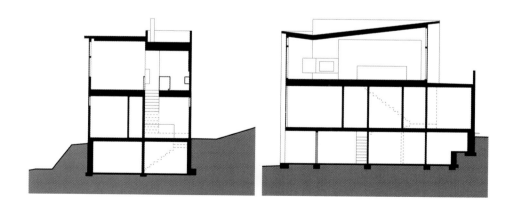

F10 HOUSE
CHICAGO, ILLINOIS
EHDD ARCHITECTURE
$120.00 PER SQUARE FOOT
2003

In 2000, before "green architecture" became a ubiquitous marketing term for architects and developers, the City of Chicago launched a design competition, Green Homes for Chicago. Its brief called for a 1,200-square-foot, energy-efficient, low-maintenance, and environmentally responsible house to be built for $200,000 on a tiny lot in Chicago's Hermosa neighborhood. EHDD Architecture submitted a winning schematic design proposal, and three years later the home was completed. The building was tagged the Factor 10 House because it was intended to reduce life-cycle environmental impacts by a factor of ten over the average contemporary American home.

Firm principal Marc L'Italien based the house on four important principles of sustainability: size reduction, improved efficiency, extended life span, and decreased environmental impact. What is remarkable about F10, as it is better known, is that EHDD achieved such a high level of sustainability in a truly affordable house. Many of the green features the architects incorporated—a passive ventilation system, solar chimney, and planted sod roof—even reduce the owners' monthly bills.

The two-story, 1,830-square-foot house, clad in red-stained fiber-cement siding has a modular, open plan that maximizes natural cross ventilation. The solar chimney brings light and air into the center of the loftlike living spaces and is supplemented by a fan that pulls warm air up and out of the house in the summer and pushes warm air down into the house in the winter, obviating the need for central air conditioning. Insulation is unusual and visually appealing: EHDD installed a floor-to-ceiling wall of recycled plastic bottles filled with Chicago tap water to create a heat sink. The functional display is a clever and whimsical addition to the stark, white interior. Another thoughtful touch is the rooftop herb garden, which is nourished by storm water runoff. In order to squeeze as much living space as possible into the skinny 125-by-125-foot urban lot, the architect opted not to construct a garage. L'Italien sees these moves as reinterpretations of history: "Our low-tech, energy-saving concepts are not radical or new; we simply reinvented strategies used in residential buildings at the turn of the twentieth century."

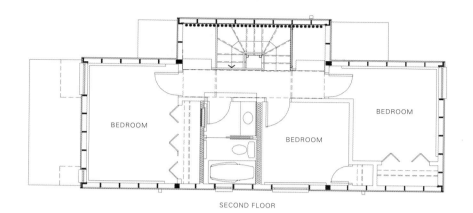

SECOND FLOOR

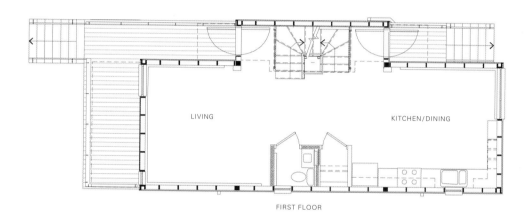

FIRST FLOOR

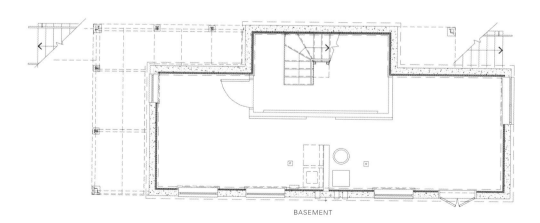

BASEMENT

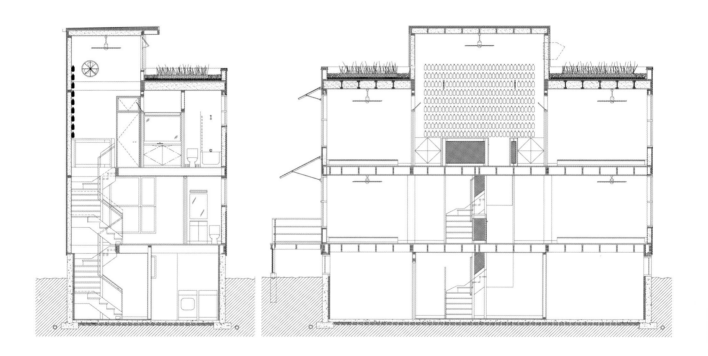

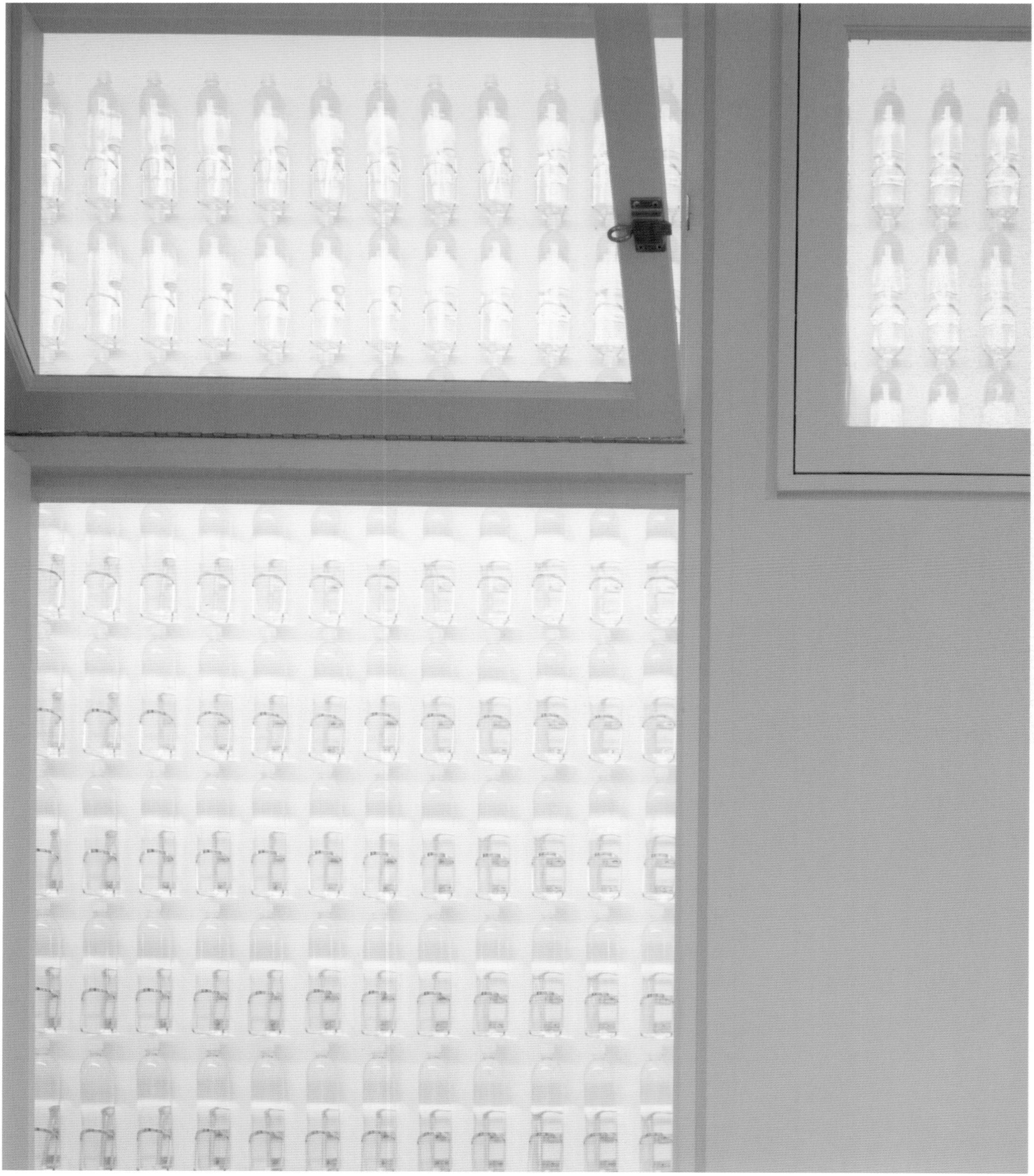

PRIOLEAU WALKER RESIDENCE
CHARLOTTE, NORTH CAROLINA
RICKENBACKER + LEUNG
$130.00 PER SQUARE FOOT
2006

"I wanted this building to appear as an integral part of the landscape, to rest gently on the land, to almost disappear," states architect Shawn Rickenbacker of New York–based firm Rickenbacker + Leung, who designed this 3,000-square-foot, three-bedroom house in rural North Carolina. The house is a calm, cerebral composition, elegantly clad in silvery cedar, but it was not exactly what Rickenbacker's demanding clients—his mother and stepfather—first had in mind. He remembers, "They kept asking me what color the house would be when it was already finished!" It is lucky that, in the end, his folks trusted his judgment. The residence is spacious, sophisticated, and complex; it is suitable for a couple retiring to the pastoral southern countryside after a lifetime of living in Manhattan skyscrapers.

Rickenbacker + Leung sited the house in a natural clearing, positioning the building with the surrounding woods and daily path of the sun in mind. Opaque and transparent materials—glass, cedar, and stone—alternate on the genteel facade, hinting at the spatial layering inside. To accommodate a specific request for private contemplative space on the exterior of the building, the architect included three terraces on the second story, each facing a different direction. Upper-level windows are positioned strategically to reveal distinct views. On the ground floor, a wall of commercial storefront windows and sliding doors opens to the expansive outdoors. The public rooms on the ground floor are organized in a linear fashion and topped by a series of interlocking, dramatically cantilevered volumes that comprise the private quarters above.

Costs were kept to a minimum by using a commercial contractor rather than a traditional residential contractor. The architect chose to incorporate local building techniques, reducing the odds of expensive construction mistakes. Only environmentally responsible materials such as bamboo flooring, cement fiber panels, and natural cedar were used.

MASTER
BEDROOM

CLOSET

CLOSET

BEDROOM

OPEN TO BELOW

TERRACE

LIBRARY

TERRACE

SECOND FLOOR

TERRACE

FAMILY
ROOM

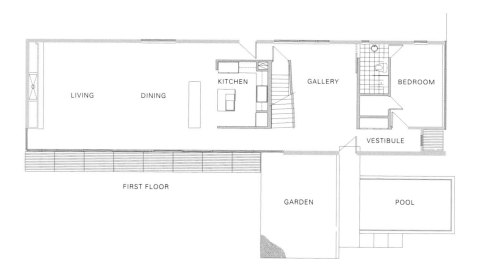

LIVING

DINING

KITCHEN

GALLERY

BEDROOM

VESTIBULE

FIRST FLOOR

GARDEN

POOL

SUGAR CREEK RESIDENCE
AUSTIN, TEXAS
KRDB
$150.00 PER SQUARE FOOT
2006

Scenic clusters of oak and cedar trees peppered picturesquely across this rolling hill determined the siting and layout for the 2,500-square-foot Sugar Creek Residence. Located at the foot of Hill Country, the single-story house nestles on the top of a rise with a dramatic view of the wooded ravine below. The L-shaped building, which contains three bedrooms, two and a half baths, and an attached music room, gently wraps around and celebrates three juvenile oak trees on the one-acre lot.

KRDB (Krager Robertson Design Build) has joined a growing nationwide trend in structuring its office as a design/build corporation, and served as both architect and general contractor on this project. Value-engineering tests conducted while the house's schematic design evolved revealed the most cost-effective building options. Chris Krager, founder and principal, reckoned that keeping the entire process with the firm—rather than bidding out to different contractors—saved his client 20 to 25 percent on construction. KRDB is also a national distributor for Gerkin Windows and Doors, and offered this client substantial discounts on commercial-grade storefront windows. These savings allowed the firm to incorporate expensive materials, fine finishes, and custom woodwork into the design, including birch cabinets in the kitchen and living areas and mahogany bathroom vanities.

An industrial aesthetic defines both the interior and exterior. The structural system was designed as a hybrid of steel framework and metal-clad insulated panels that provides a very tight, energy-efficient envelope that offers long-term savings. The panel system, although expensive in itself, also offered a measure of modularity, smoothing the framing process. Consequently, labor costs were reduced: it took only one and a half weeks to erect rather than the more typical six weeks. Durable concrete block and painted panels complete the downtown look and require minimal maintenance.

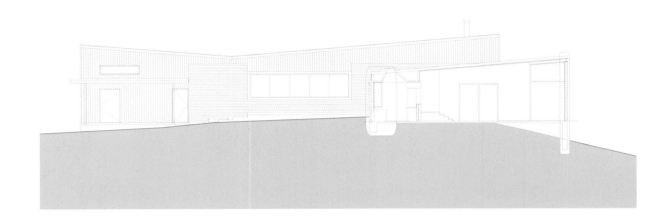

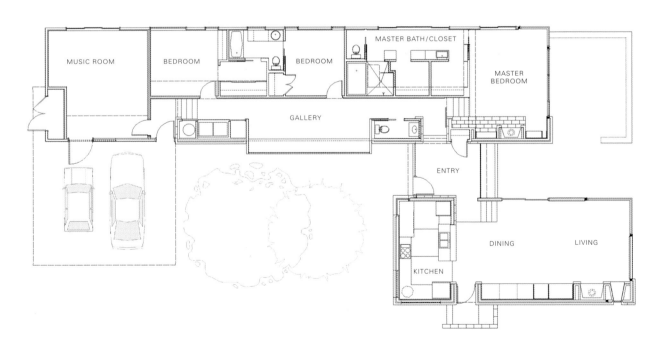

MUSIC ROOM

BEDROOM

BEDROOM

MASTER BATH/CLOSET

MASTER BEDROOM

GALLERY

ENTRY

DINING

LIVING

KITCHEN

FORT GREENE HOUSE
BROOKLYN, NEW YORK
CHRISTOFF:FINIO ARCHITECTURE
$150.00 PER SQUARE FOOT
2004

Fort Greene, a trendy quarter of Brooklyn, sits sandwiched in between two very different neighborhoods—posh and established Brooklyn Heights and up-and-coming Bedford-Stuyvesant, where a disproportionately high number of rap and hip-hop artists, including Jay-Z, Lil' Kim, and Busta Rhymes, have grown up. Real estate prices in the Fort Greene neighborhood have been skyrocketing, making the 20-by-80-foot vacant lot this new home was built on a rare and precious find. The owners, a jewelry designer and a music producer, hired Martin Finio and Taryn Christoff of Christoff:Finio architecture to design the residence on a very tight budget.

The architects decided to hang the floors of the new house from the existing, adjacent townhouse walls. This reduced construction costs considerably: there was no need to invest in insulation, additional framing, or cladding. The exposed—but washed and sealed—brick-and-plaster walls punctuated by naked ducts, pipes, and electrical conduits create a loftlike industrial feel. Savings in this area stretched the budget to allow for a luxuriously sized house, four stories high, with a total of 4,200 square feet of living and working space.

A jewelry workshop and soundproof recording studio occupy the basement and ground-floor levels. The dining area, kitchen, and a double-height living room form the second floor; the third, technically a mezzanine, overlooks these spaces. Three bedrooms, two bathrooms, and the laundry room are all housed on the topmost level. Circulation is stacked vertically along the southern side of the house.

Simple details and finishes also kept costs low. Aluminum-magnesium commercial railings were used on the staircases, and raw plywood became inexpensive flooring. Industrial baseboard heaters were cheap to buy and install and enhance the project's overall aesthetic. Brick found on the site was recycled for use on the smart-looking facade, and large-scale commercial storefront windows cleverly placed along both of its vertical edges maximize natural light in the interior while maintaining privacy. The entire home possesses a delightful contemporary appearance. The front blends perfectly into the traditional brownstone neighborhood, but it is by far the sexiest house on the block.

THIRD FLOOR

MEZZANINE

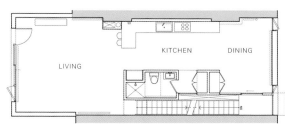

SECOND FLOOR

FIRST FLOOR

BASEMENT

IDEAL HOUSE
ANCHORAGE, ALASKA
MAYER SATTLER-SMITH ARCHITECTS
$150.00 PER SQUARE FOOT
2007

Architectural firm Mayer Sattler-Smith applied the forward-looking strategy of planning for future needs in the ingenious design for the Ideal House, the winning entry in an affordable housing competition held by the Cook Inlet Housing Authority. This one-story, long, narrow shoebox house is structurally prepared for easy and affordable upward expansion. Modular segments can be attached to the flat roof to form a second story, doubling the home's size and ensuring that additions will not encroach on precious backyard space.

The contest called for a cost-effective, energy-efficient, and low-maintenance home to be built on a 50-by-125-foot lot. Mayer Sattler-Smith's design provides 1,300 square feet of living space and was conceived as a family-friendly project: physical and visual flow between the indoors and the outdoors allows parents to monitor children, as evidenced in the openness of the layout and the well-defined relationship between the garden and the home. Light infuses all primary living spaces, and backyard activity can easily be observed from inside the house, a rare planning consideration in the northern setting of Alaska.

The chic interior with unusually high ceilings is creatively organized, with flexible rooms that can accommodate more than

one program. Mayer Sattler-Smith divided the house according to three distinct "activity zones." Three bedrooms, a bathroom, and a study comprise the private zone. The public zone accommodates group activities—eating, playing, and entertaining—and is situated for easy flow to the outside. The utility zone includes a mudroom, laundry room, and garage and also has windows, allowing natural light to permeate the workspaces.

Environmentally friendly materials and methods were used throughout. The foundation is concrete slab on grade, and the house itself is fabricated with structural insulated panels clad with local, rough-hewn cottonwood siding. These 8-by-24-foot wall panels replace standard 2-by-6-foot construction frames, providing superior insulation by eliminating the need for seams and studs; their ability to prevent typical drafts that cause heat loss makes them 30 percent more energy efficient than conventional frames. The concrete floors emit radiant heat, which in conjunction with the interior's white reflective walls and large, south-facing glass-and-vinyl windows, help save on energy costs. An eye to the future is apparent even in the stark wooden siding, which will eventually weather to an attractive silvery hue, eliminating future painting expenses.

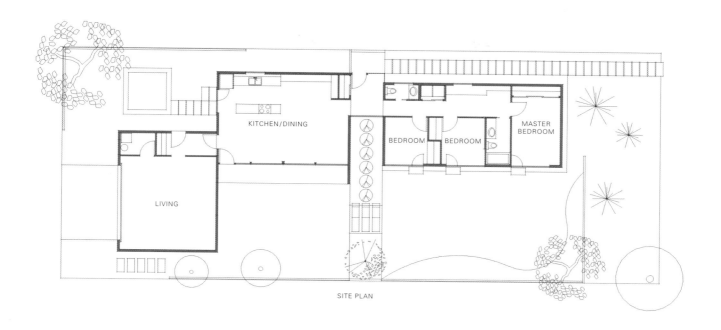

KITCHEN/DINING

LIVING

BEDROOM BEDROOM MASTER
BEDROOM

SITE PLAN

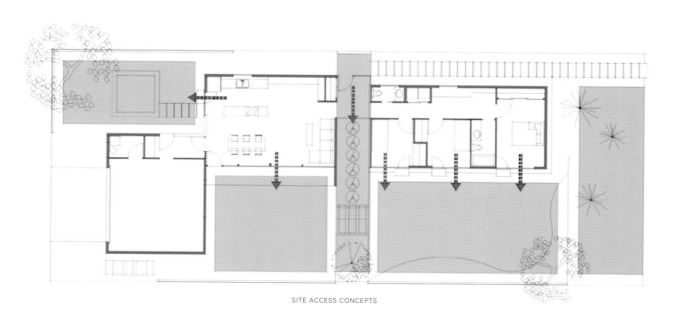

SITE ACCESS CONCEPTS

MILAN HOUSE
MILAN, NEW YORK
WILLIAM MASSIE ARCHITECT
$172.00 PER SQUARE FOOT
2007

The production of important and innovative residential architecture has historically required an enlightened client who is interested in experimentation. The cutting-edge design for Milan House, set on six acres of scenic forest in upstate New York, was made possible by a contemporary champion of the avant-garde: Greg Wooten, co-owner of the twentieth-century design store Mondo Cane in New York City. Wooten collaborated with William Massie on the interior of his Tribeca store and later commissioned him to design and build an affordable vacation house.

Wooten was amenable to letting Massie conceive of his house as part of the architect's ongoing research project at the Cranbrook Academy of Art in Michigan. Massie's work is centered around an unusual fabrication technique: large project-specific component parts, including wood, steel, and acrylic elements, were produced off-site in a custom, state-of-the-art laser-cutting workshop in Detroit before being shipped to the construction site. Architecture students from Cranbrook assisted with the house's construction, living at the site and sleeping outdoors in all seasons to complete the majority of the detailed assembly work. While free labor saved on construction costs, the intense level of detailing—even the dimmer switches are laser-cut—and untested manufacturing

procedures meant that the projected schedule of one year dragged into four years of continuous labor, but Wooten was committed to maintaining the purity of Massie's vision. The craftsmanship and patience the graduate students brought to the job, which they claim "required enormous, spontaneous, human ingenuity," enabled the dramatic result.

The house ingeniously balances a 1960s-mod feel and a peaceful getaway ambience. The 1,800-square-foot house is a simple rectilinear volume that contains kitchen, living, and dining spaces. Two bedroom/bathroom spaces are located at each end of the rectangular plan, and neither is completely closed off from the main space.

"I envisioned the entire house as though it were a rubber box in the act of being squeezed," says Massie. The house appears to have been squashed at either end, as though someone sat on it, creating an intriguing juxtaposition of curves and angles; it looks like poured concrete but is really skim-coated, laminated timber. Unexpected round wall surfaces and an oddly shaped fenestration resulting from the alternately concave and convex exterior also add voluptuous animation to the interior. Acrylic windows, which sit in 4-inch-thick steel frames lacquered with chocolate-colored

boat varnish, were individually gun-glued in place and run the length of the house. Striations of amber acrylic lined with inexpensive Electro Tape are layered in these deep frames, and glow in the sunlight. This rich color is echoed in the cherry-plywood walls, designed and installed as pieces of a puzzle, complete with zigzagged perimeters.

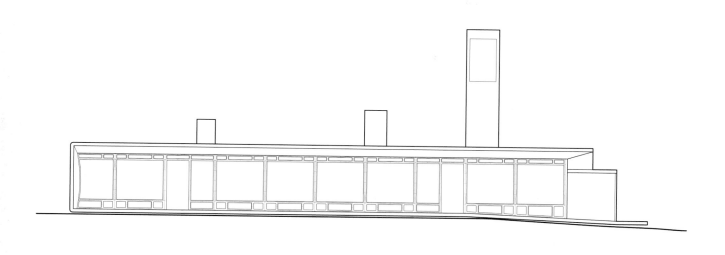

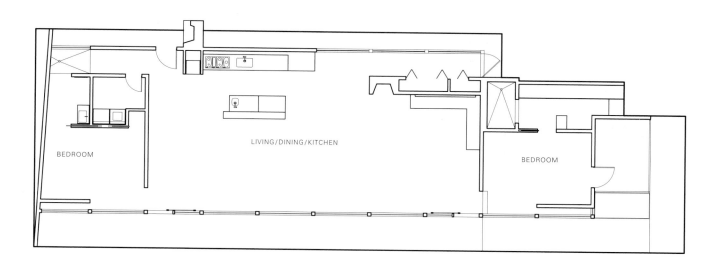

BEDROOM

LIVING/DINING/KITCHEN

BEDROOM

UPCHER HOUSE
EAST HAMPTON, NEW YORK
BATES MASI ARCHITECTS
$190.00 PER SQUARE FOOT
2005

"When designing within a budget, it is essential to understand what the client views as the project's single most important element," says Paul Masi of Bates Masi Architects. "In this case it was adaptability." The client, a British novelist, wanted a flexible, year-round house that could contain her collection of over 2,000 books. When considering the excessive load-bearing requirements for this weight, Masi conceived of a house built on a giant, adjustable cantilevering rack system of the kind frequently employed in lumberyards.

"You find solutions that you would never even have looked for if you had more money," explains Masi. The elegant structural system, fabricated of black-painted vertical steel columns with prepunched holes, an assortment of adjustable steel brackets, and movable steel arms, supports the flat roof, the second floor, kitchen cabinetry, handrails, and both interior and exterior lighting. A mahogany catwalk that provides access to the library is also hung from these supports. The entire interior skeleton, which allows each element it supports to be raised or lowered, was purchased and built for $7,000. The Upcher House can easily be adapted, retrofitted, expanded, or reduced by manipulating this clever outsized rack system.

The efficiency of the structure is echoed in the simple, square footprint of the house. The overall 1,400-square-foot floor plan is organized around one large, double-height room for living and dining. Two bedrooms, two bathrooms, a study, the library, and two outdoor decks emanate from this central area. Construction costs were kept to a minimum by incorporating inexpensive materials such as green-tinted fiberboard for the exterior cladding, rough-sawn okoume wood, aluminum-frame windows, preassembled wood screens, industrial cedar planks for the bookshelves, Ikea kitchen cabinets (also used as medicine cabinets in the bathrooms), and kitchen appliances from General Electric.

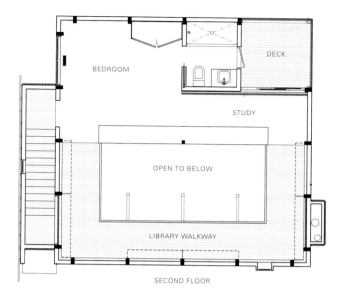

BEDROOM

DECK

STUDY

OPEN TO BELOW

LIBRARY WALKWAY

SECOND FLOOR

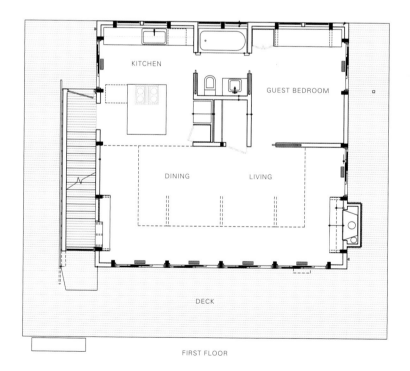

KITCHEN

GUEST BEDROOM

DINING   LIVING

DECK

FIRST FLOOR

18TH STREET HOUSE
BROOKLYN, NEW YORK
BANGIA AGOSTINHO
$195.00 PER SQUARE FOOT
2006

This light and airy gem of a house sits sandwiched between two narrow, mid-nineteenth century wood-frame townhouses on a jam-packed block in the rather gritty Brooklyn neighborhood of South Park Slope. The project's designers, Anshu Bangia and William Agostinho with George R. Restivo, reversed the standard ratio of glass to wall to create an interior with a sunny, capacious feel by day, and an exterior that glows by night. Sets of 6-by-8-foot floor-to-ceiling windows on both the front and rear facades make the building seem transparent. When the sunshades are up, a passerby can look straight through the 42-foot-long house to the garden.

Owner David Petersen, a documentary filmmaker, hired friends Bangia and Agostinho to complete what he initially believed would be a straightforward, low-budget renovation of an existing 1,100-square-foot house. The project quickly turned into a nightmare: soon after the interior was gutted, it was discovered that the exterior walls were a mere 5 inches thick and extremely unstable, the original roof was sagging, and the existing foundations were crumbling. With no feasible way to rectify these structural faults, the team concluded that it would be necessary to build an entirely new house.

The cheapest way to accomplish this was to leave the too-thin sidewalls intact. Bangia Agostinho constructed a new light-gauge, freestanding, structural-steel box inside the old walls; this is essentially a new house with independent walls built within the old, oddly slanting walls. Although this resulted in a narrow interior—just 12 feet 6 inches—Bangia Agostinho added a third story that also boasts a 13-by-13-foot terrace for a total of 1,500 square feet. All mechanical elements were housed in the new 600-square-foot basement. The designers' solution to circulation, staggering the stacked stairs to one side, creates a remarkably efficient layout. The living room has a double-height ceiling that further opens up the slender space. A small balcony off the staircase overlooks this room, adding to the drama of the space. With their client's limited budget in mind, the designers chose cost-effective materials: floors are standard 4-by-8-foot maple plywood sheets, prefabricated cabinetry from Ikea is used in the kitchen, and the cedar windows and doors were purchased from a Canadian company called Bonneville. The exterior is covered in cedar siding that blends well with the neighboring houses. These two young designers very cleverly manipulated space to replace a dilapidated, tilting wreck with a spectacular urban glass house.

KITCHEN

LIVING/DINING

FIRST FLOOR

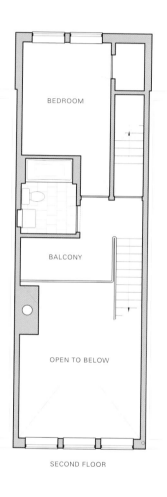

BEDROOM

BALCONY

OPEN TO BELOW

SECOND FLOOR

BEDROOM

OFFICE

DECK

THIRD FLOOR

FIELD HOUSE
ELLINGTON, WISCONSIN
WENDELL BURNETTE ARCHITECTS
$200.00 PER SQUARE FOOT
2004

Field House, a beautiful, large vacation home in Wisconsin's Fox River Valley, is aptly named for its spectacular agrarian setting. Located on the highest point of a gently sloping 16-acre farm property, the house is surrounded by newly planted apple, pear, and plum orchards and fields of seasonally rotating crops—wheat, corn, soybeans, alfalfa, and oats grown to supply nearby dairy farms. Although a high-end, luxury home, Field House, commissioned by an oncologist working on the East Coast, was relatively inexpensive to build. This was due to a meticulous, efficient design and the involvement of a quality commercial builder as the general contractor.

The 5,000-square-foot building is essentially a 24-by-96-by-32-foot box clad in galvanized zinc. The designer of the house, architect Wendell Burnette, took inspiration from local buildings: grain silos, dairy barns, and tool sheds. All the materials that are part of the house, including the dramatic rolled-metal siding, were utilized in their existing standard dimensions. "I am interested in the notion of economy, of using standard products to achieve elegance in unexpected, different ways," professes Burnette. Erecting this structure required commercial construction techniques rather than traditional residential building methods.

After completing the schematic design phase, Burnette interviewed two local contractors. Miron Construction, the biggest contractor in Wisconsin, won the job, although this was only the second house the company had ever constructed. Burnette says he was "impressed with the workmanship and the Wisconsin work ethic."

The materials and the neutral color palette add to the calm, peaceful aura of the site. White limestone masonry, standard block from nearby quarries, draws the visitor in; the same limestone serves as gravel on the drive and entranceway. The floor is simple black concrete, and the main door is cedar. Walls and ceilings are mill-finished, oiled steel, and built-in cabinetry is American black walnut. The rooftop, the owners' private sanctuary, has a secret observatory reached by a silo ladder. This silvery wooden oasis has no railings past a certain point, and the only deck furniture is an iconic white Marc Newson chair floating in the landscape, not unlike this house that floats in a sea of fields.

GALLERY

KITCHEN

DRESSING

SCREEN
PORCH

MASTER
BEDROOM

LIBRARY/
STUDY

GYM

DINING   LIVING

FIREPIT

SECOND FLOOR

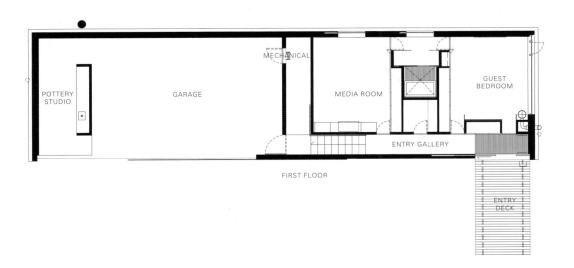

MECHANICAL

POTTERY
STUDIO

GARAGE

MEDIA ROOM

GUEST
BEDROOM

ENTRY GALLERY

FIRST FLOOR

ENTRY
DECK

NEWFIELD HOUSE
NEWFIELD, NEW YORK
CENTRAL OFFICE OF ARCHITECTURE
$200.00 PER SQUARE FOOT
2002

The Newfield residence, a weekend home in rustic upstate New York, is a startlingly fresh hybrid that merges three distinct styles: classic suburban ranch, open-plan loft, and local garden shed. The architectural firm for the project, Central Office of Architecture, based in Los Angeles, has created an unexpectedly seductive house with an unyielding modernist sense of efficiency and rationality.

The one-bedroom, two-bathroom, 2,400-square-foot house is improbably simple: it is essentially a long, rectangular bar anchored by a garage at one end and an outdoor deck on the other. Uninterrupted windows echo the horizontal form of this glorified, perfectly proportioned shed. The fenestration runs the length of both sides, imparting a spacious feeling and creating a tangible relationship between the rather spartan interior and the surrounding, lush 14-acre forest and the wild turkeys, woodchucks, and deer that live there.

Inside, the architects designed a continuous counter fabricated from black epoxy resin—frequently used in medical laboratories—below the continuous ribbon window on the north wall. This surface, a strong horizontal datum, changes function as it stretches the length of the house—it serves successively as office desk, kitchen counter, living room display shelf, cabinet, and bedroom dresser.

The glass-and-steel house was designed to require a minimum amount of maintenance over time. The floor, part of the flat concrete slab foundation that made construction easier and less costly, is fitted with radiant heating, and the metal siding and aluminum windows require little upkeep.

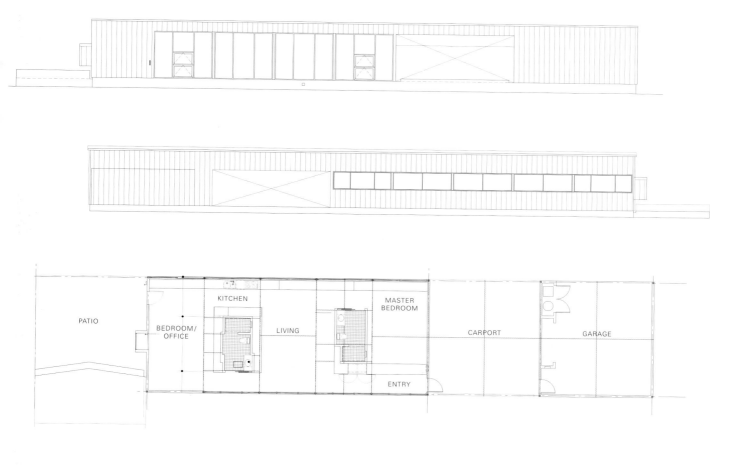

PATIO

BEDROOM/
OFFICE

KITCHEN

LIVING

MASTER
BEDROOM

ENTRY

CARPORT

GARAGE

BIG DIG HOUSE
LEXINGTON, MASSACHUSETTS
SINGLE SPEED DESIGN
$200.00 PER SQUARE FOOT
2006

Architects John Hong and Jinhee Park of Single Speed Design and their client Paul Pedini, a structural engineer, collaborated on the Big Dig House, a 3,800-square-foot, single-family home. The premise behind this pioneering architectural experiment was simple and straightforward: to recycle and reuse pieces of the temporary infrastructure of Boston's Central Artery/Tunnel Project, unofficially known as the Big Dig. Single Speed Design salvaged oversized steel and concrete composite pieces from demolished I-93 off-ramps and used them without modification as the structure and skin of the house.

These reclaimed materials, weighing in at an extraordinary 600,000 pounds, were used primarily as found to keep labor costs at a minimum. They were not cut or altered in any substantial way. The environmental impact of this gesture is significant, as these pieces would have otherwise been discarded. Cost savings for Pedini were also significant, about $50 per square foot, spread across both materials and labor. Sweat equity and considerable brain equity also reduced the cost of this house. Pedini's wife, a water resources engineer, devised a water reuse strategy for the home and served as the project manager on a day-to-day basis.

Large-scale and weighty highway components withstand much higher loads than conventional building elements; this fact informed the house's design and fabrication. Despite the necessity of paying high rental fees for the cranes needed to place the heavy reused pieces of concrete and steel once they arrived at the site, the owner ultimately saved on construction costs. Assembly took days rather than weeks. According to Hong, "The framing structure was in place in nineteen hours, a process that usually takes a minimum of six weeks if it involves timber and studs."

Here, exterior walls are not load bearing, as is customary in traditional residential architecture, allowing for large expanses of uninterrupted glass such as the dramatic strip of horizontal windows that wraps around the kitchen and living area. Substantial panels of reinforced-concrete roadway are also sturdy enough to support three feet of soil, so a large roof garden was created, adding to the list of the building's sustainable features. A salvaged concrete cistern collects runoff rainwater underground, which is used to maintain the roofscape.

The graceful three-bedroom, three-bathroom house is located in a cul-de-sac on the perimeter of an illustrious

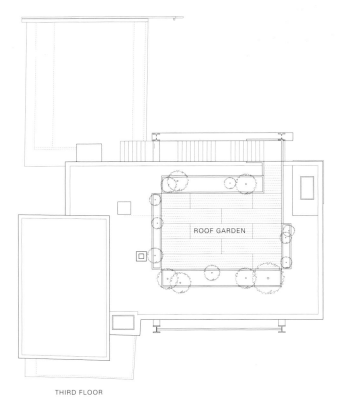

THIRD FLOOR

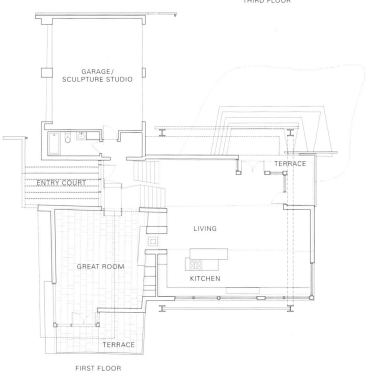

GARAGE/
SCULPTURE STUDIO

ENTRY COURT

TERRACE

LIVING

GREAT ROOM

KITCHEN

TERRACE

FIRST FLOOR

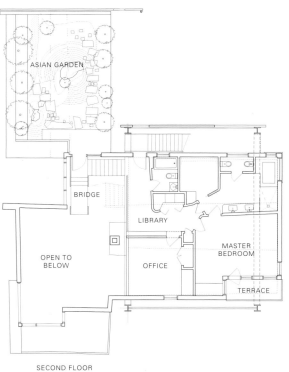

ASIAN GARDEN

BRIDGE

LIBRARY

OPEN TO
BELOW

OFFICE

MASTER
BEDROOM

TERRACE

SECOND FLOOR

neighborhood: the Six Moon Hill community founded in 1947 by the Architects Collaborative. Early schematics for the house underwent many changes to meet the criteria for new construction. "The board guidelines did not allow for a lot of freedom. We had originally wanted to design along with the highway's trapezoidal forms, but our design took on modernist language. It became a more polite house," Hong says. Despite many challenges, the Big Dig House became a rigorously beautiful, inventive, and thought-provoking project, based on an idea as ambitious as the construction project that inspired it.

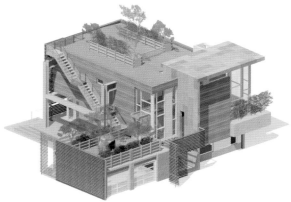

DUANE STREET RESIDENCE
LOS ANGELES, CALIFORNIA
CHASEN ARCHITECTURE
$220.00 PER SQUARE FOOT
2006

Architect and general contractor Greg Chasen, founder of Chasen Architecture, purchased this tiny 27.5-by-125-foot hillside site very cheaply, then faced the challenge of designing and building a reasonably sized house on it without incurring prohibitive costs for the foundation. In order to meet California's rigorous geotechnical engineering code, Chasen had to remove an enormous amount of sandstone—the slope averaged 50 percent, or about 30 degrees for 90 feet of the depth of the lot—and then replace it with an equally enormous amount of poured concrete. Site preparation alone amounted to a quarter of the final construction budget and took four months to complete.

The streamlined house has been thoughtfully pieced together, negotiating the steep slope seamlessly. Two large, landscaped patios mitigate the change of grade, and concrete block stairs wrap theatrically around the exterior of the building, making the house a natural setting for parties. Chasen opted to incorporate the ground level into the house rather than to use it as a garage as originally intended, relegating parking to the outdoors; this brought the total living space to three stories and 1,700 square feet.

Chasen chose cost-effective materials throughout. A timber-frame structure is elegantly exposed at certain points throughout the house. Durable cement board, Hardipanel, and metal siding form the cladding, which is fastened with air space behind it to allow moisture to escape and prolong the life of the wooden frame. Windows are strategically and economically placed—few are included on the front facade or lower level to enhance privacy and provide security in the gritty urban neighborhood. Instead, upper-level apertures overlook the patios and enhance the hilltop view. Environmentally responsible reclaimed Douglas fir, bought directly from a northern California mill, is reminiscent of the region's Arts and Crafts tradition.

Chasen performed much of the labor himself, including cutting the Hardipanel that he had purchased at Home Depot, and screwing all of the 2,000 screws that attach it to the frame. He also mixed exterior paint into custom colors that blend beautifully with the local agave and eucalyptus plants, determined the random yet rhythmic pattern for the facade, and painted the entire building. This took considerably longer than hiring a crew, but Chasen was meticulous about the building's finishes. From this experience he advises, "A material might be cheap, but if it is difficult to install, it becomes a trade-off, not a savings. It is important to devise an installation system that is simple and fast."

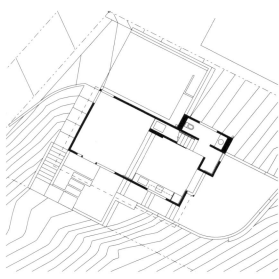

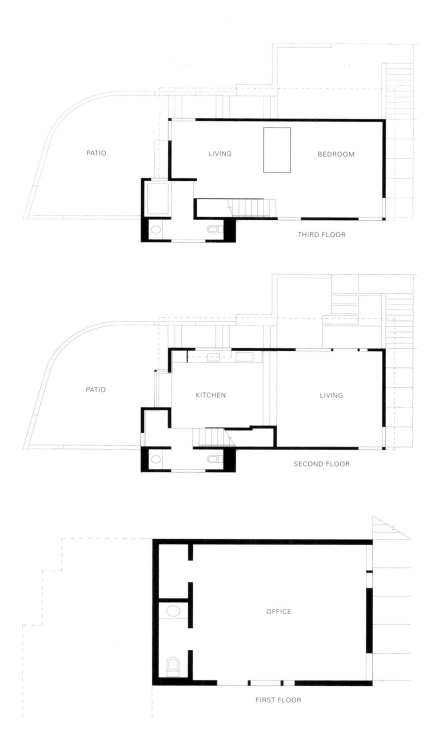

PATIO   LIVING   BEDROOM

THIRD FLOOR

PATIO   KITCHEN   LIVING

SECOND FLOOR

OFFICE

FIRST FLOOR

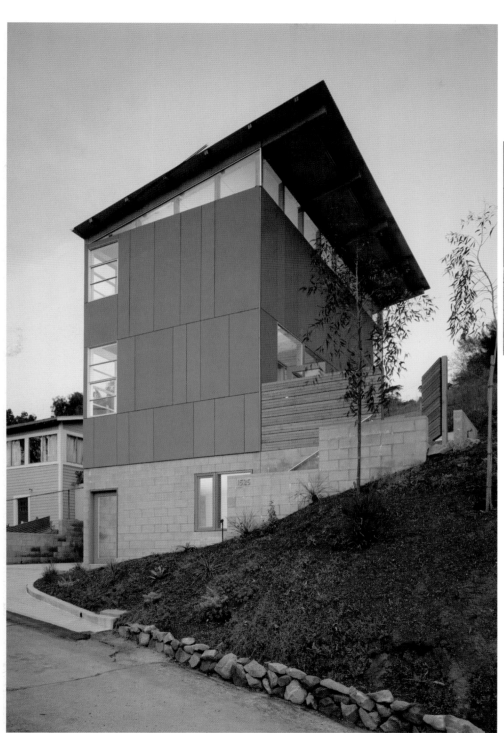

BESTOR HOUSE
ECHO PARK HILLS, CALIFORNIA
BARBARA BESTOR ARCHITECTURE
$220.00 PER SQUARE FOOT
2005

Architect Barbara Bestor was not only the designer but also the general contractor and original owner of this charming, 1,200-square-foot house in Echo Park Hills. Since Bestor played all three roles necessary in development, she was able to economize in significant ways. The entire project is an improvisational riff on well-established design/build strategies where, customarily, a budget is developed, schematic illustrations and floor plans are drawn, and detailed construction documents are given to a contractor. Bestor saved time and money by calculating budgets herself, envisioning the spatial layout in her head, and employing a builder who had worked with her eponymous firm for years and knew her methods well enough to forego paperwork. Her fortuitous individualization of the project "allowed me total control over the entire process," said Bestor.

A second significant cost-saving maneuver Bestor choreographed was to preserve the original timber beams of the dilapidated 1920s cabin sitting on the quarter-acre lot. Rather than knock it down and start anew, incurring additional costs, Bestor preserved the original wooden framework and built a new foundation around the old house's structural shell.

Bestor managed to shave her budget down a third way: by using inexpensive materials for both structural elements and finish details. The roof is galvanized aluminum; it cost just $5000 and requires no upkeep. Hardiplank, an inexpensive fiber-cement board, is used as cladding. Bestor painted this surprisingly attractive material a dramatic bluish black, making the home's large expanses of glass—on which she saved over $20,000 by purchasing commercial-grade rather than residential windows—glow at night.

The fire pit, fishpond, and outdoor seating area are all poured concrete and cost $1,500. Square concrete pavers were purchased for $3 each. On the interior, Bestor finished the walls of her daughters' room with plywood panels and hung hospital tracks with brightly colored Marimekko fabric curtains to divide the space.Bathroom walls are lined with waterproof, mildewproof corrugated PVC that is manufactured for use in garden sheds. Bright red vintage airplane seat fabric covers her sturdy living room sofa, and in her adjacent home office, strikingly unusual custom-colored wallpaper by graphic artist Geoff McFetridge, a friend, frames the outdoor greenscape.

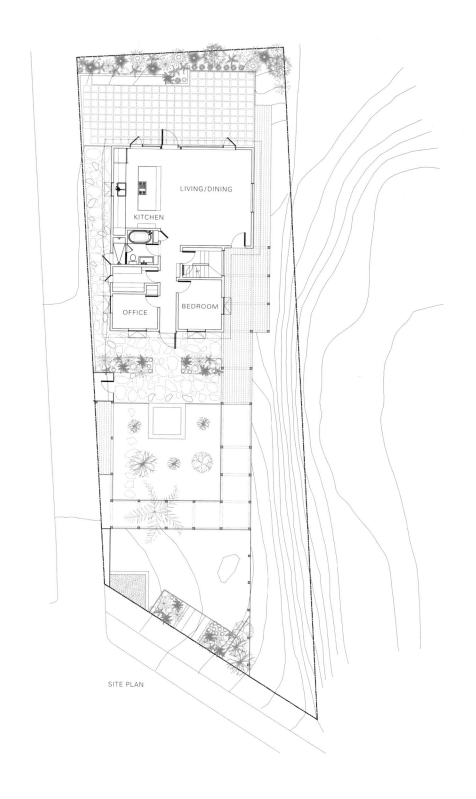

LIVING/DINING

KITCHEN

OFFICE

BEDROOM

SITE PLAN

PHOTOGRAPHY CREDITS

Numbers refer to page numbers.

ABOUT THE AUTHOR

Susanna Sirefman is the founder and principal of Dovetail Design
Strategists LLC, a firm that matches clients with designers,
architects, and landscape architects. She is the author of several
books, including *New York: A Guide to Recent Architecture,
Chicago: A Guide to Recent Architecture, Whereabouts: New
Architecture with Local Identities*, and *The Contemporary
Guesthouse: Building in the Garden*; has contributed to
Architecture, Architectural Record, Metropolis, and *Graphis;*
and is currently a contributing editor for *Surface*. Sirefman
trained at the Architectural Association School of Architecture
in London before returning to her native New York, where she
has taught at the Parsons School of Design and at the School
of Architecture, Urban Design and Landscape Architecture at
the City College of New York. She was recently an advisor for
"Urban Voids: Grounds for Change," an international design
competition for Philadelphia's vacant land sponsored by the Van
Alen Institute and the City Parks Association of Philadelphia.